D1553512

Colin
Powell

Read These Other
Ferguson Career Biographies

Maya Angelou
Author and
Documentary Filmmaker
by Lucia Raatma

Leonard Bernstein
Composer and Conductor
by Jean F. Blashfield

Shirley Temple Black
Actor and Diplomat
by Jean F. Blashfield

George Bush
Business Executive
and U.S. President
by Robert Green

Bill Gates
Computer Programmer
and Entrepreneur
by Lucia Raatma

John Glenn
Astronaut and U.S. Senator
by Robert Green

Martin Luther King Jr.
Minister and
Civil Rights Activist
by Brendan January

Charles Lindbergh
Pilot
by Lucia Raatma

Sandra Day O'Connor
Lawyer and
Supreme Court Justice
by Jean Kinney Williams

Wilma Rudolph
Athlete and Educator
by Alice K. Flanagan

FERGUSON
CAREER BIOGRAPHIES

Colin
Powell

U.S. General and Secretary of State

BY ALICE K. FLANAGAN

Ferguson Publishing Company
Chicago, Illinois

Photographs ©: Reuters NewMedia Inc./Corbis, cover; Lisa Quinones/Black Star, 8; Barry King/Liaison Agency, 11; Underwood & Underwood/Corbis, 14; Mike Albans/AP/Wide World Photos, 19; AP/Wide World Photos, 22; Schwartz Collection/Archive Photos, 26; Arthur Rothstein/Corbis, 29; Dennis Brack/Black Star, 32; Bettmann/Corbis, 36; Victor Malafronte/Archive Photos, 40; John Harrington/Black Star, 44; Bettmann/Corbis, 50; AP/Wide World Photos, 56; Leif Skoogfors/Corbis, 58; Charles Tasnadi/AP/Wide World Photos, 61; AP/Wide World Photos, 65; Bettmann/Corbis, 68; Ira Schwarz/AP/Wide World Photos, 72; Vince Mannino/Bettmann/Corbis, 76; Joe Marquette/AP/Wide World Photos, 78; Bettmann/Corbis, 81; Helene C. Stikkel/AP/Wide World Photos, 83; Doug Mills/AP/Wide World Photos, 85; Greg English/AP/Wide World Photos, 87; Dennis Brack/Black Star, 88; Greg Gibson/AP/Wide World Photos, 90; Reuters/Steve Jaffe/Bettmann/Corbis, 93; Sasa Kralj/AP/Wide World Photos, 94; Reuters/Jay Gorodetzer/Archive Photos, 98; Reuters/Mark Wilson/Archive Photos, 100.

An Editorial Directions Book

Library of Congress Cataloging-in-Publication Data
Flanagan, Alice K.
    Colin Powell / by Alice K. Flanagan.
    p. cm. — (Ferguson career biographies)
    Includes bibliographical references and index.
    ISBN 0-89434-372-6
    1.Powell, Colin L.—Juvenile literature. 2. Generals—United States—Biography—Juvenile literature. 3. Afro-American generals—Biography—Juvenile literature. 4. United States. Army—Biography—Juvenile literature. [1. Powell, Colin L. 2. Generals. 3. Afro-Americans—Biography.] I. Title. II. Ferguson's career biographies.
E840.8.P64 F58 2001
355'.0092—dc21   00-048400

Copyright © 2001 by Ferguson Publishing Company
Published and distributed by
Ferguson Publishing Company
200 West Jackson Boulevard, Suite 700
Chicago, Illinois 60606
www.fergpubco.com

Printed in the United States of America
Y-3

CONTENTS

Colin
Powell

Role model. Colin Powell's success comes from hard work and a sense of responsibility.

FAMILY COMES FIRST

Four-star General Colin Powell was once called a "tough-as-nails military man with compassion and soul." Powell was the first African-American to serve as chairman of the Joint Chiefs of Staff, the highest U.S. military group. His journey to power in the White House began in the streets of New York's Harlem where dreams have difficult starts.

Although Colin Powell was neither an exceptional child nor a promising student, his life changed dramatically when he discovered his talents and turned them into skills. Colin Powell's story is about character and family, duty and responsibility. It is a story of brotherhood and faith. His life teaches us that the road to success begins with discovering what interests us. Excelling in life takes education, hard work, and the will to use what we have learned. Few people have done it so well. Colin Powell's life is an inspiration to us all.

Pride and Hope

A bright, silver star shone in the New York sky on April 5, 1937, the day Colin Luther Powell was born. His parents, Maud Ariel McKoy Powell and Luther Theophilus Powell, were exceptionally proud of their only son.

Colin's parents immigrated to the United States from Jamaica in their early twenties, hoping to create a better life for themselves and their families. In the 1920s, Maud Ariel McKoy joined her mother in Harlem, New York, where they both found work as dressmakers. Luther Theophilus Powell arrived in Philadelphia in 1920 and then moved to Connecticut, where he worked as a gardener. Later, he moved to New York City where he became a building superintendent and then a stock boy for a clothing com-

Alma and Colin Powell. Devotion to family is an important part of Powell's life.

pany called Ginsburg's. Eventually, Luther Powell worked his way up from stock boy to shipping clerk and finally to foreman of the shipping department. Even at his highest-paying job, however, he never earned more than $60 a week.

Parents Set the Example

Luther Powell was a short man, about 5 feet 2 inches (157 centimeters) tall. Although he was small in stature, he had a big heart. He was kind and caring and often brought total strangers home for dinner. Although Luther Powell was a man of few words, he had a commanding personality. He liked order and was almost never seen in public without a suit and tie. Education was important to him even though he quit high school when he was a boy to help support his family. Faith was also important to him. He was active in the Episcopal Church throughout his life and served as senior warden, an important leader in his parish.

Colin's mother, Maud Powell, was also hardworking and religious. In addition to working at the clothing factory, she took care of the household and volunteered at church. Maud was proud that she had completed high school. She enjoyed supervising her children's schoolwork and keeping them in line.

Colin often said: "She could cut me down with a single glance."

The Powells had a strong sense of family. They helped one another and sacrificed for one another. When Colin grew up and looked back on his life, he praised his parents for the way they raised him. He said: "My heroes are my parents, Luther and Maud Powell. As I get older, I find I have a greater and greater appreciation for what my parents did for me. They set a wonderful example, demonstrating love and care and sacrifice for my sister and me, as well as my many cousins. In their own quiet way they made it clear that there were certain expectations of each of us. That meant getting educated, getting a job, and going as far as you could with that job."

Luther and Maud met in the summer of 1927. After a two-year courtship, they married on December 28, 1929. The couple moved into an apartment building at 20 Morningside Avenue in Harlem, a fashionable African-American neighborhood at the time. Their first child, Marilyn, was born here in 1931. Their son, Colin, came along 5 1/2 years later. By that time the neighborhood was beginning to change, and it became clear that it was no longer a safe place to raise children.

Harlem in the 1920s. Young Colin lived here before he and his family moved to the Bronx.

Growing Up in the Bronx

In 1943, when Colin was six years old, the family moved from Harlem to the South Bronx in New York City. They rented a four-bedroom apartment at 952 Kelly Street in a community called Hunt's Point. It was a working-class neighborhood made up of a variety of races and nationalities. Though heavily Jewish at that time, the community eventually included families from Mexico, Puerto Rico, China, Ireland, Poland, Italy, and several African countries. In the neighborhood, everybody knew everybody's business.

Colin and his sister, Marilyn, grew up in a large, extended family. It included Colin, Marilyn, and their parents, plus their mom's sister, brother, and mother. A host of other family members lived within a four-block radius. Colin's Aunt Gytha and Uncle Alfred Coote lived across the street from them, and Colin passed his Aunt Laurice and Uncle Vic's house on the way to school. A little farther down, his godmother lived with her family. His Aunt Beryl also lived nearby.

A Close-Knit Family

This close-knit family of aunts, uncles, and cousins watched over Colin and his sister. Throughout Colin's life, these family ties provided the strength, security, and support he needed to be happy and successful.

The people and places important to Colin were all within walking distance of his house. His grade school was three blocks away, and if he walked another block, he reached his junior high school. Between the two schools stood St. Margaret's Episcopal Church, where the family had its own pew. And a few blocks in the opposite direction was Colin's high school. As Colin Powell put it, "When I stepped out the door onto Kelly Street, I saw my whole world."

Colin played in the streets with children of various racial backgrounds. They made up most of their games, which usually involved balls and marbles. Kite-flying on the roofs of the tenements was a popular pastime, and so was bicycle riding. But their favorite activity was "making the walk." That's what Colin and his friends called walking around the neighborhood. The "walk" included passing the Jewish bakery, the Puerto Rican grocery store, the Chinese laundry, the Italian butcher shop, the movie theater, and several candy stores. Every nationality, including Jamaicans, had a specialty store where you could buy food and clothing from that country.

Over time, Hunt's Point changed and Kelly Street became a dangerous place to live—the neighborhood was plagued with drugs and violence. Colin saw many of the kids he grew up with go to jail—or die. Fortunately, he managed to keep out of trouble and stay away from drugs.

Colin once told a group of high school students why he stayed clear of drugs: "One, my parents would have killed me, but the second reason is that . . . it was stupid. It was the most self-destructive thing you could do with the life that God and your parents had given to you."

A Happy-Go-Lucky Kid

In school, Colin was well liked and had a lot of friends. He was a pleasant and cooperative student, but his grades were mediocre. Colin worked just hard enough to pass to the next grade. Nothing seemed to interest him very much. He took piano lessons, and later studied the flute, but never went any further with the studies.

Even in high school, Colin found little to spark his enthusiasm. He wasn't much of an athlete. He joined the basketball team at St. Margaret's, but after spending most of his time on the bench, he quit. In his junior year at Morris High School, he won a letter in track but then he got bored and quit the team.

Colin's study habits didn't fare much better. He was more interested in building things and taking them apart than in studying. Colin graduated from Morris High School with a C average. In later years, he wrote about this time in his life. He said, "I lacked drive, not ability. I was a happy-go-lucky kid, amenable, amiable, and aimless."

What Colin lacked in personal goals, however, he made up in friendships that lasted from grade school into adulthood. Colin often said that when he was growing up, his best times were "hanging out with the guys, and 'making the walk' from Kelly Street, up 163rd Street around Southern Boulevard to Westchester Avenue, and back home. Our Saturday-morning rite was to go to the Tiffany Theater and watch the serial and then a double feature of cowboy movies."

Colin's inability to stick to anything worried his parents, who valued education, responsibility, and hard work. They probably wondered when their son was going to find his niche in life and excel. They were pleased when he became an altar boy and sub-deacon at St. Margaret's Episcopal Church. His per-

Returning to his roots. Powell has taken time to speak with students at Morris High School, his alma mater.

sonality seemed to thrive there in the structured atmosphere of church pageantry and tradition.

Colin's parents were even more delighted when their son, at the age of fourteen, began working steadily at Sickser's furniture store. Previously, Colin had worked at a variety of jobs to earn pocket money, but this was the first job he showed serious interest in. After school and on weekends, he unloaded trucks and fixed cribs and baby carriages for the Jewish storeowner who lived a couple of blocks from the Powells' home.

Colin graduated from high school in February 1954, at the age of sixteen. As a result of the school's accelerated program, he met the requirements for graduation in just 3 1/2 years. He was glad to be finished with high school and wasn't looking forward to continuing his education. However, he didn't want to disappoint his parents.

As he said, "I went to college for a single reason: My parents expected it. I don't recall having had any great urge to get a higher education. I don't even remember consciously thinking the matter through."

Following in his sister's footsteps, and in accordance with his parents' wishes, Colin enrolled in college. Initially, two schools had accepted him: New York University (NYU) and the City College of New York (CCNY). Colin chose CCNY because the tuition was cheaper—NYU charged $750 a year and CCNY charged only $10.

In uniform. Powell enjoyed the discipline of the military and soon realized he was suited to army life.

PREPARING FOR A MILITARY CAREER

When Colin enrolled as a freshman at CCNY, he was not sure what he wanted to study. At the urging of his mother, he decided to major in engineering. "That's where the money is," his mother told him. So Colin gave it his best, averaging a B in the first semester. But the field of engineering held little interest for Colin. He had neither the natural ability nor the motivation to develop the skills necessary to make a career of it. By the end of the year, he decided to change his major.

Building Character through Hard Work

While in college, Colin continued to work at Sickser's store on weekends and during the Christmas season. But when the school year ended, he got a better-paying job at a Pepsi-Cola bottling plant.

Colin got ninety cents an hour to mop floors at the bottling plant. Unlike many young men his age, he didn't think mopping floors was beneath his dignity, and he wasn't embarrassed by it. In fact, he learned that there was a technique to mopping floors. Colin actually learned the technique and turned it into an opportunity for a promotion. Later in life, he talked about mopping floors: "If that was what I had to do to earn $65 a week, I'd do it. I'd mop the place until it glowed in the dark. Whatever skill the job required, I soon mastered. You mop from side to side, not back and forth, unless you want to break your back." Colin's ability to master skills and then use them to help him advance to another job served him well throughout his life.

The foreman at the Pepsi-Cola plant was impressed with Colin's work habits and promised to let him work on the bottling machine the following summer. (All the workers on the bottling machines were white. All the workers who mopped floors were black.) When Colin returned to the plant the next summer, he became one of the best line inspectors on the machines. By the end of the third summer, he was deputy shift leader.

While working at the Pepsi-Cola bottling plant, Colin learned a valuable lesson. "All work is honorable. Always do your best, because someone is watching." This lesson, learned so early in life, was one of the major reasons for Colin Powell's successful career.

Learning Discipline

In the fall of 1954, Colin changed his major from engineering to geology. He thought geology might be easier for him, but it wasn't. Colin didn't have a strong interest in any of the sciences. He enjoyed the field trips though, and managed to get a few As in his courses by the time he graduated.

Colin might never have made it through college had it not been for a life-altering discovery he made during his first semester. One day on campus, he saw a group of young men in military uniforms. They were cadets in the Reserve Officers Training Corps (ROTC). The ROTC prepares students for a future in military service. After train-

POSNER, STANLEY   3093 Brighton 4 St., Bklyn. 35
POTACK, FREDERIC   1780 Bryant Ave., Bx. 60
POWELL, COLIN L.   183-68 Elmira Ave., Qns. 12
    House Plan; ROTC: Pershing Rifles President, Cadet's
    cer's Club.

POWERS, CATHERINE   250 W. 99 St., N. Y. 25
    Art Society: Secretary.
PROFFITT, PETER D.   87-77 94 St., Qns. 21   B
    ASME; SAE.
PYRPYRIS, VLASSIOS   410 Riverside Dr., N. Y. 25   B
    Chi Epsilon; ASCE; Carroll Brown Hellenic Society.

RABINOWITZ, HELEN   615 Pelham Pkwy., Bx. 67
    Hillel: Recording Secretary, Chorus Chmn.; Alpha
    Delta: Treasurer, President.
RABINOWITZ, HENRY   33-27 75 St., Qns. 72
    Biological Review: Editorial Staff; Caduceus Society
RAFTEN, BARRY   4865 Broadway, N. Y. 34   B.
    Pi Tau Sigma.

From the City College yearbook. Powell (upper right) gained a lot from his college experience.

ing in the ROTC, cadets often enter the military as officers.

Colin Powell was immediately attracted to the uniforms and the disciplined lifestyle of the ROTC. Not long after enquiring about the organization, he enrolled in it. Later, when asked why he enrolled, Powell said, "At this point, not a single Kelly Street friend of mine was going to college. I was seventeen. I felt cut off and lonely. The uniform gave me a sense of belonging, and something I had never experienced all the while I was growing up; I felt distinctive."

That fall, Colin Powell joined the Pershing Rifles drill team, one of the more dedicated units within the ROTC. According to Colin, "The Pershing Rifles were a little more serious than the average ROTC cadets." And that appealed to him. Also, the members of the Pershing Rifles came from different ethnic and financial backgrounds, but race, religion, and financial background never mattered to these cadets. They drilled together and partied together. They stood up for one another like brothers.

As a cadet, Colin learned basic infantry tactics, army procedures, and rifle marksmanship. He became skilled at reading maps and performing drills and ceremonies. As leader of his unit, he rose quickly to the top of his class, inspiring others to do their best as well.

A Sense of Belonging

Nothing Colin Powell had experienced thus far in high school or on basketball and track teams had given him a feeling of belonging. But now, as a cadet, he understood what brotherhood meant. He seemed to crave the discipline, structure, and companionship of the Pershing Rifles. Their selflessness reminded him of the caring atmosphere within his family.

For the first time in his life, Colin had found something that he was really good at—soldiering. It motivated him to excel and enabled him to set the kind of goals he wanted to reach.

The "Best Cadet"

During the summer of 1957, Colin spent six weeks training with other cadets at an ROTC camp in Fort Bragg, North Carolina. He learned to shoot a rifle, drill troops, and how to camouflage and set up road-blocks. At the end of the six weeks, the cadets were judged on their course grades, rifle-range scores, physical fitness, and leadership ability. Colin received outstanding marks. He was named "Best Cadet, Company D" and second-best cadet for the entire camp. This was the highest honor any black cadet had ever achieved at the camp.

Colin was ecstatic about the honor and should have returned home bragging about a perfect summer. But on the night of his last day in camp, he was told that he had been denied first-place honor because he was black. That night, Colin learned about discrimination firsthand. Although he felt hurt by the prejudice of others, he didn't allow it to affect his behavior negatively. Instead,

Soldiers at Fort Bragg. In 1957, Powell spent six weeks at an ROTC camp at this army base.

the experience made him more determined than ever to succeed.

On the day Colin was named Best Cadet, he was also given a pen set with those words engraved on it. When he returned home and showed it to his parents, he was proud of himself. As Colin Powell said in his autobiography, "I was bringing my parents something they had never had from me—proof, with my desk set, that I had at last excelled. And I had found something that I did well. I could lead. The discovery was no small gift for a young man at age twenty."

For the next thirty-five years, Colin Powell carried the pen set with him to every job. He kept it on his desk in the White House when he was national security adviser and at the Pentagon when he was chairman of the Joint Chiefs of Staff. To this day, it remains a permanent reminder of an important experience in self-discovery.

Cadet Colonel Colin Powell

Cadet Colin Powell returned to college energized. Although he continued doing just enough to get by academically, he got straight As in ROTC. When he graduated in 1958, he averaged only a C. Yet he had achieved the highest rank in the ROTC—cadet colonel—and was named the distinguished military graduate of his group.

On June 9, 1958, Colin Powell strode past his parents in the auditorium and declared, "I, Colin Luther Powell, do solemnly swear that I will support and defend the Constitution of the United States against all enemies foreign and domestic and that I will well and faithfully discharge the duties of the office upon which I am about to enter, so help me God." The next day, Colin Powell graduated from college. As a distinguished military graduate, he was offered a regular commission in the army rather than a commission in the army reserve. Powell was happy to accept the army commission and the three years of active duty that accompanied it.

On June 30, 1958, he became a second lieutenant in the U.S. Army. A few days later, he said good-bye to his family and friends and headed for Fort Benning, Georgia, for basic training. Colin's parents expected their son to serve the required three years and then return to New York and get a real job. But Colin, who loved being a soldier, would spend the next thirty-five years of his life in the army, serving his country with all his heart.

Strong character. Powell is a good leader because he sets high standards for himself.

LEADING BY EXAMPLE

When Second Lieutenant Colin Luther Powell began basic training in June 1958, his pay was $220 a month. The first two weeks were physically demanding. They were purposely designed to weed out the weak soldiers before ranger training began. Powell learned that the best infantry officers were skilled rangers and paratroopers. They could serve in any capacity because they were ready for any combat situation. Powell knew that to be the best infantry officer he could be, he would first have to become a good ranger and paratrooper.

Powell had little difficulty meeting the challenges of the first two weeks of basic training and finished in the top ten of his class. By the time the course was over, he had made the infantry officer's code of conduct his own, which he summarized as follows: "The infantry officer was to go into battle up front, demonstrating courage, determination, strength, proficiency, and selfless sacrifice." Only then would he ask his men to follow him. As part of the officers' training, Powell said: "We were to march into hell, if necessary, to accomplish the mission. At the same time, we were taught to fulfill this responsibility while trying to keep ourselves and our men from being killed."

Meeting Racism Head-On

When Colin Powell enrolled in the ROTC at age seventeen, he met young men who trained together, challenged one another as equals, and cared for one another like brothers, regardless of their differences. He learned that each person's rank, or standing in the group, was based on a merit system—on what they could achieve. During his training as a soldier and an officer, Powell's understanding of brotherhood deepened. He learned the extent to which brothers are willing to sacrifice for each other, no matter what.

Every time Powell left the army base and went into town, however, this sense of brotherhood was replaced with the reality of racism. In town, blacks were separated from other Americans in public places. There were separate drinking fountains and restrooms for blacks and for whites as well as separate sections in buses and restaurants. Few opportunities were offered to blacks because blacks were judged not on merit but simply on the color of their skin. As Powell recalled in his autobiography, "I could go into Woolworth's in Columbus, Georgia, and buy anything I wanted, as long as I did not try to eat there. I could go into a department store and they would take my money, as long as I did not try to use the men's room."

Powell developed a way to cope with racism. Each time he experienced it, he thought about the military and how it offered him opportunities to excel. He kept his focus there, where he believed he would be judged on merit, not on race.

Instead of becoming angry with the people who discriminated against him, Powell treated the experience as a challenge. He said: "If people in the South insisted on living by crazy rules, then I would play the hand dealt me for now. If I was to be confined to

Separate drinking fountains. Off the army base, Powell experienced racial discrimination just as other African-Americans did.

one end of the playing field, then I was going to be a star on that part of the field. Nothing that happened off-post, none of the indignities, none of the injustices, was going to inhibit my performance. I was not going to let myself become emotionally crippled because I could not play on the whole field. I did not feel inferior, and I was not going to let anybody make me believe I was. I was not going to allow someone else's feelings about me to become my feelings about myself. . . . I occasionally felt hurt; I felt anger; but most of all I felt challenged."

Ranger and Airborne Training

Challenge was what becoming a ranger was all about. Powell spent the first half of his ranger training in the hot Florida swamps. For two months, he learned how to live in the heat and the water and eat rattlesnake and alligator meat to survive. The second half of ranger training took him to northern Georgia for mountain training. There he lived outdoors, scaling cliffs, patroling at night in hip-deep water, and sleeping on the ground. Ranger training taught Colin Powell more than wilderness survival and combat skills, however. It also taught him loyalty, selfless service, and responsibility.

Following ranger training, Powell reported for airborne training. Physically, he was exhausted and suffering from a leg infection that he had picked up sliding down one of the mountains. But mentally, he was charged and ready to go. Rather than let doctors look at the infection, he treated it himself so that he wouldn't be held back while it healed.

For the next several weeks, Powell learned to parachute from planes, fight without weapons, and survive in the wilderness. He conquered his fears of physical danger and found the success exhilarating. Before every test, he asked himself the questions every soldier asks himself: "Do I have physical courage?" "Do I have what I need to conquer my fears and do what needs to be done?" As Powell passed each test with courage, he knew in his heart that he had what it took to be an airborne ranger. In January 1958, he received his paratrooper wings and the black-and-gold ranger tabs. He was now ready to be a soldier and an officer in the field.

First Field Command

Powell's first orders sent him to Gelnhausen, an American outpost about 25 miles (40 kilometers) east of Frankfurt, Germany. At that time, there was a threat of war between the United States and the Soviet Union. The Soviet military zone was only 43 miles (69 km) to the east. In the event of a war with the Soviet Union, this was the spot the U.S. Army believed Soviet troops might come through on their way into Europe.

Powell's unit, Combat Command B of the Third Armored Division, occupied Coleman Kaserne, a former German army post near the Vogelsberg Mountains. There, twenty-one-year-old Powell began his first command—as a platoon leader of forty men in Company B (Bravo Command), Second Armored Rifle Battalion, Forty-eighth Infantry.

Through the bitter German winter and hot summer, Powell sat in his M59 armored personnel carrier with eleven other soldiers guarding the border.

They kept watch for signs of Soviet troop movements. It was a boring job, but important nonetheless. And Powell took his first command of soldiers very seriously. He said: "These men were not my buddies; they were my responsibility. I was to take care of them."

Powell's superiors called him "a fine platoon leader" and promoted him to first lieutenant in December 1959. In November 1960, Powell completed his assignment and was sent back to the United States.

Powell spent the next two years at Fort Devens, Massachusetts, with the Fifth Infantry Division. The Fifth was a mechanized infantry unit. Briefly, Powell was executive officer of Company A and then company commander. Finally, he became adjutant of a new unit, the First Battalion, Second Infantry, which paid him $290 a month.

By the summer of 1961, Powell had finished his three years of service and was eligible to go home as a civilian. He could return to New York to work with his father in the garment district or pursue a career in geology. For Powell, neither of these was an option. He loved being a soldier and decided to reenlist. This decision would change his life drastically.

Husband and wife. Over the years, Alma has been a supportive partner in all of General Powell's efforts.

LOVE AND WAR

4

Change came one November day in 1961. A friend of Colin's had contacted him at Fort Devens to ask him for a favor. His buddy asked him to join him on a date with two college girls. It would be a foursome. Colin was not going out with any girl at the time and thought it might be fun to go out with his buddy and his buddy's girlfriend. But he had never met the girl who was supposed to be his date and he was not about to risk having a miserable time with her, so Colin backed out.

Eventually, however, his friendship for his buddy won out, and Colin agreed to go on the blind date. It turned out to be a fortunate decision for Colin. That night he met Alma Vivian Johnson, the woman who eventually became his wife.

At the first sight of his date's lovely green eyes, Colin was hooked. He was also attracted to her soft southern accent and graceful movement. During one of their long conversations, he learned that Alma had been born and raised in Birmingham, Alabama. She had moved to Boston, Massachusetts, to do graduate work in audiology—the study of hearing.

At the time Colin met Alma, she was working as an audiologist for the Boston Guild for the Hard of Hearing. She drove a large van to various sites and gave people hearing tests.

About one month and several dates later, Colin asked Alma to meet his folks. She joined him in New York at a family New Year's Eve party. Alma liked the loving group of people she met and she had no trouble fitting in. Although she was neither a Jamaican nor a New Yorker, Colin's family accepted Alma warmly and welcomed her as a member of their family.

After Colin returned to Fort Devens, Alma began

visiting him on weekends. She met all his friends and got a better picture of army life. She and Colin soon became inseparable and felt they must be in love. In August 1962, Colin received his orders to go to Vietnam, a country in Southeast Asia. For a year, Colin Powell would be advising and training South Vietnamese military.

Alma did not share Colin's enthusiasm for his assignment. She was afraid their separation from each other would change their relationship. She gave him an ultimatum: either make a commitment to her before he left for Vietnam or end their relationship.

Shocked by Alma's reaction, Colin was forced to face what was in his heart. He knew that he and his family loved Alma and that she would make a wonderful wife. Colin decided to propose to Alma. Two weeks later, they were married.

Marriage

Colin and Alma were married on August 25, 1962, in Birmingham, Alabama. Both families attended the wedding. It was a hectic time. Colin remembers: "We got married on a Saturday, spent the night in Birmingham, flew back to Boston on a Sunday, and I was

Through good times and bad. Colin and Alma were married shortly before Colin left for Vietnam.

at work Monday." Colin's parents held a wedding reception for them not long afterward in New York.

The newlyweds had about four months together before Colin, recently promoted to the rank of captain, had to leave for Vietnam. A month after the wedding, they flew to Fort Bragg, North Carolina. Colin attended a six-week training course to prepare for Vietnam while Alma unpacked their things and settled down in the one room they would share in the home of some friends. After Colin's training was over, he and Alma celebrated Christmas early. Then he took a plane to Vietnam and Alma flew back to Birmingham to spend the year with her parents. She was expecting a baby, and they would help her in the months ahead.

At the time, Birmingham was a hotbed of racial violence. For many years, African-Americans had fought against laws that forced them into second-class citizenship. In the 1950s, they participated in peaceful protest marches against segregation laws that kept black and white Americans separate. Alma's family lived outside central Birmingham but still in a dangerous area. During this time of unrest, her father often stood watch at the window with a shotgun.

While Colin was in Vietnam, Alma wrote to him often. But she never shared news about the civil rights struggle at home. She felt that he had enough to deal with in Vietnam. After Colin returned from Vietnam and learned of the situation, he was troubled that he wasn't able to take part in the civil rights movement in the United States. He did, however, participate in the struggle in his own way. By his example, Colin showed other black soldiers that it was possible to advance through hard work and a positive attitude. "Because of my position," Colin said, "and the things I was doing in my life, I didn't have a chance to participate in that struggle in an active way. I did it in my own way, by my own example and by helping other people who were coming along as best I could."

First Tour of Duty in Vietnam

Captain Colin Powell arrived in South Vietnam on Christmas morning, 1962, at the height of the rainy season. At the time, two warring armies were locked in battle. Both wanted sole control of the small country of Vietnam. The communist forces in the North were receiving aid from China, and the democratic forces in the South were receiving aid from the United States.

Captain Powell quickly acquainted himself with the base camp and the Vietnamese officers in charge of the 400-man Second Battalion, Third Infantry Regiment, of the First Division. He learned that the camp's mission was to protect an airstrip that received incoming supplies for the war.

Throughout the next few months, Powell provided military advice. He trained the Vietnamese soldiers to shoot rifles, taught them patrol tactics, and helped with disciplinary problems. He often accompanied the soldiers on patrol through jungle terrain filled with snakes, leeches, and swarms of insects. The patrols, like sitting ducks, were constantly ambushed by enemy snipers.

For Captain Powell, this was a dangerous but exciting time. His training in the Florida swamps and Georgia mountains was finally proving useful. His excitement turned to fear and sadness, however, when he encountered his first battle and saw soldiers die. Afterward, he was glad to be alive but felt guilty that he had survived while others had not.

One day in July 1963, Powell experienced his own brush with death. It happened while his unit was headed to a Special Forces camp for rest. They were marching along a creek bed when Powell stepped into an enemy booby trap called a punji-stick trap. It was made of sharpened bamboo sticks buried in the ground. The points, which stuck out, were poisoned with buffalo dung. One of the sticks pierced Powell's boot and penetrated the sole of his foot. Although he was in terrible pain, Powell managed to grab a branch to use as a crutch and keep moving. After arriving in camp, he was taken to a hospital for surgery. Powell recovered quickly but spent the remaining months as an assistant adviser on the operations staff at headquarters.

By November 1, Powell's tour of duty was over and he headed home. Two medals awaited him: the Purple Heart, given to soldiers wounded in action, and the Bronze Star, for bravery.

Fatherhood

While Powell was serving in Vietnam, Alma had given birth to a baby boy. Their son, Michael Kevin Powell, was born on March 23, 1963. News of his birth finally reached Powell in Vietnam almost three weeks later. The reality of being a father hit Powell hard. He felt responsible for the new life he had helped bring into the world and was determined to get back home safely.

Powell returned to the United States on November 22, 1963. Alma was waiting for him at the Birmingham airport in his old blue Volkswagen. After a joyous reunion, he and Alma quickly got reacquainted and caught up on family news. The Volkswagen headed for a homecoming feast at Alma's parents' home. Later, Colin, Alma, and the baby drove to New York to spend Christmas with the Powell clan.

The Little Brick House on Twenty-eighth Avenue

After he returned from Vietnam, Colin Powell was assigned to Fort Benning, Georgia, where he would take the Infantry Officers Advanced Course (IOAC). Because he didn't have to report to Fort Benning until August 1964, Colin had plenty of time to find a house and get it in shape for his family. He found a small brick house in Phenix City, Alabama, about 10 miles (16 km) from Fort Benning. The house on Twenty-eighth Avenue was the first home the Powells would share as a family. It has since become famous. In 1993, Twenty-eighth Avenue was renamed General Colin L. Powell Parkway.

Nearby, a drive-in hamburger joint became notorious. It was the place that refused service to Colin Powell in 1963 because of his race. One evening, before Alma and Michael had moved into their home on Twenty-eighth Avenue, Colin had stopped at a roadside restaurant to order a hamburger. He knew he would be refused service inside the restaurant, so he parked the car and ordered from his car window. When the waitress realized that Colin Powell was black, she refused to serve him. He would have to come to the back window, she said. Colin

African-American protestors in Alabama. The Powells continued to feel the effects of racism in the 1960s.

drove away angry, thinking about how he had risked his life for his country in Vietnam but couldn't get a hamburger in a U.S. restaurant.

Colin Powell didn't allow himself to stay angry for long, however. He thought about the importance of his career and hurried to the officers' club at the post, where he knew he would be served just like everybody else.

Over the next eight months, Powell took advanced airborne ranger training to become an elite paratrooper, known as a pathfinder. Following the training, he became an equipment test officer for the Infantry Board. By the time the infantry course began at Fort Benning, Powell was wearing the pathfinder insignia next to his combat infantryman's badge, airborne wings, and ranger tab. And he had promised to reapply for the job of Infantry Board testing officer at Benning after the career course was over.

The Infantry Officers Advanced Course prepared infantry captains to take over command of a company and to serve on the battalion staff. The IOAC was a required course for officers most likely to make a career of the army. Powell completed the course in May 1965, ranking first among infantrymen and third in the class overall. He also became certified in the use of tactical nuclear weapons. But one event for him stood out above all others. Colin Powell received his greatest thrill as a father, when his second child, Linda, was born on April 16, 1965.

As promised, Powell returned to the Infantry Board after the career course. But in the spring of 1966, he was called back to infantry school, this time as an instructor. After going through an intense instructor's course, Powell began teaching students ranging from officer candidates to reserve generals. He taught amphibious operations (land, sea, and air maneuvers) and trained officer candidates who were shipping out to Vietnam as second lieutenants in the infantry.

Attending College at Fort Leavenworth

In May 1966, twenty-nine-year-old Powell was promoted to major and chosen to attend the army's Command and General Staff College (CGSC) at Fort Leavenworth, Kansas. CGSC was a prestigious school. Only the best officers from around the world attended it. At the college, Powell took advanced training for army commanders, which included how to plan military campaigns. He graduated second out of 1,244 students, thus adding one more honor to his impressive accomplishments.

Colin and Alma Powell couldn't have been happier at Leavenworth. Their life was pleasant and secure. But all that soon changed. Shortly after graduating, Colin Powell received his new assignment—a second tour of duty in Vietnam. Alma was devastated by the news but accepted the fact that her husband was a professional soldier and had to go wherever and whenever he was sent. For Colin, who was now a father, this separation would be harder than the first one.

Colin and Alma agreed that she and the children would live in Birmingham, near Alma's family, while he was gone. Feeling confident that his family would be cared for, Colin left for Vietnam.

Second Tour of Duty in Vietnam

On July 21, 1968, Colin Powell began his second tour of duty. This time, however, it was as Major Colin Powell, executive officer of the Third Battalion, First Infantry Regiment, Eleventh Infantry Brigade of the Twenty-third Infantry Division known as the Americal Division.

Major Colin Powell's job was to make sure his battalion of 800 men had all the support they needed to remain in excellent fighting condition. That meant everything from ordering ammunition to getting mail to the troops. Four months into Powell's tour, however, he was unexpectedly taken out of action and promoted to the division's assistant chief of staff.

The commander of the Twenty-third Infantry, Major General Charles M. Gettys, had read an article in the *Army Times* about the top five students of a recent graduating class at Leavenworth. He recognized Colin Powell as one of the graduates and realized that Powell was serving in his division. Believing that Powell's talents were not being utilized well, Gettys had Powell transferred to his staff. He made him the operations and planning officer for the division. Within days, Powell was planning warfare for nearly 18,000 troops, artillery units, aviation battalions, and a fleet of 450 helicopters! It was supposed to be a safer job. But it wasn't.

On the morning of November 16, 1968, Powell boarded a helicopter with General Gettys and other important military staff. They were going to visit several North Vietnamese Army camps that had recently been captured by the Eleventh Infantry Brigade. While heading toward the site, the helicopter clipped a tree and crashed to the ground. Powell stumbled out of the smoking wreckage, limping on a broken ankle, then returned and risked his life to rescue General Gettys and other soldiers. For his bravery, Powell received the Soldier's Medal.

At the base hospital, doctors put Powell's ankle in a cast and sent him back to work. When his tour of duty ended in July 1969, he returned to the United

States. At age thirty-two, Powell was already a highly decorated officer. So his subsequent approval to attend the army's graduate-school program came as no surprise.

Graduate School and the Pentagon

Powell enrolled at George Washington University in Washington, D.C., in the master of business administration (MBA) program. He and Alma immediately started house-hunting. They bought a home in Dale City, Virginia, with a VA loan and $20 down, $259 a month. The following year, the Powell's third child, Annemarie, was born and Colin was promoted to lieutenant colonel. Life was good.

In 1971, Powell earned his master's degree in business administration. Although his instructors encouraged him to go on for a Ph.D., Powell was tired of student life. He wanted to get back into action.

The army assigned Powell to work with General William DePuy at the Pentagon. (The Pentagon is the headquarters of the Department of Defense. The U.S. military leadership has its offices there.) DePuy knew about Powell's excellent communication skills and put him to work on his speeches.

At the Pentagon. During the time that they worked together, General William DePuy gave Powell good advice.

While in General DePuy's employ, Powell received valuable counsel from him. One day during a heart-to-heart talk, DePuy told him: "Never become so consumed by your career that nothing is left that belongs only to you and your family. Don't allow your profession to become the whole of your existence." Powell not only appreciated DePuy's advice but also lived by it. As busy as he was, Colin Powell always made time for his family and volunteered to help out at church events.

Ready and willing. Powell has always been prepared to take on any project the army or the government has given him.

DUTY, HONOR, COUNTRY

Colin Powell was happy at his job and not looking forward to changing it anytime soon. He was proud to be working in one of the most prestigious and promising offices in the Pentagon. But the army had other plans for him.

One day in November 1971, Powell received an application form from the Army Infantry Branch for a White House Fellowship. White House fellows are bright men and women from different fields. They work in the White House for a year in one of the departments of the executive branch to gain firsthand experience in government policy-making. In the process, they meet powerful American and international leaders and participate in making policies.

White House Fellow

Powell was one of the seventeen applicants—out of 1,500—chosen to receive a fellowship in 1972. He was assigned to the Office of Management and Budget (OMB), one of the most powerful federal agencies in Washington. It oversees what happens to the government's money. Its director was Caspar W. Weinberger and his deputy was Frank Carlucci. Both men would later serve as secretaries of defense and figure prominently in Powell's career.

While at the OMB, Powell helped make policy and set goals for the military. He discovered how to use his business skills and military experience in a new way. He was asked to stay on at the OMB for another year after the first one ended, but he declined. "That was not the path I wanted," he said. "The Army was my life. . . . All I wanted was to cross over to the other side of the Potomac [River] and find out what assignments the Pentagon had for a soldier eager to command troops again."

At the Office of Management and Budget. Director Caspar Weinberger was impressed with Powell and his work.

Battalion Commander in South Korea

Lieutenant Colonel Powell soon learned that he was slated to go to South Korea as the battalion commander of the First Battalion, Thirty-second Infantry, Second Infantry Division, Eighth Army. At that time, U.S. troops were in Korea to keep peace between military forces in the North and South. In 1950, North Korean troops had invaded the South, beginning a three-year war between the two sides. United Nations (UN) forces, supported by the United States, aided the South, while China aided the North. On July 27, 1953, North Korea signed an armistice—an end to the fighting—with the UN.

Powell was excited when he received the news of his new assignment, even though he knew it would be difficult telling Alma. Korea was an "unaccompanied tour," which meant that she and the children could not come with him. This would be the third time he would be absent from their lives. Once again, he was asking them to make a sacrifice for him. And once again, they came through for him amid painful good-byes.

When Powell took command of the battalion in Korea, it was a mess. The troops lacked discipline and commitment to one another. There was racial tension, drug abuse, and low morale. Powell made changes immediately. He threw drug users in the brig, discharged unfit soldiers, and put the rest through a punishing series of tests. Before long, he had whipped the troops into shape and instilled in them a sense of duty, discipline, and responsibility for one another.

Someone once said that Powell was a "tough-as-nails military man" but he had "compassion and soul." He asked a lot from his troops, but he gave them 200 percent of himself. To Powell, the army was like a family—demanding but also supportive.

Commander of the 101st Airborne Division

While completing his year of service in Korea, Powell was chosen to attend the National War College (NWC), which is part of the National Defense University at Fort McNair in Washington, D.C. Attending a service college is the fourth and final step an officer takes in becoming a general. To Colin Powell, this was the opportunity of a lifetime.

Powell returned from Korea in September 1974. NWC classes would not start until August 1975, so Powell worked in the Pentagon for the next nine months. When classes finally began, his days were filled with lectures on the philosophy and strategy of war. In February 1976, two months before completing his course at NWC—and graduating with distinction—Powell was promoted to colonel.

Shortly after he was promoted to colonel, Powell received news that he was to take command of the Second Brigade of the famous 101st Airborne Division at Fort Campbell, Kentucky. The 101st was a helicopter assault unit made up of light infantry and helicopter battalions. Powell was put in charge of three battalions, totaling more than 2,500 men. The assignment was another step up for him. Unfortunately, it meant uprooting his family once again. Like all military families, the Powells had moved often. As Colin went from one assignment to another, he took on more responsibility while his family had to adjust to the change.

Colin and Alma sold their house in Dale City and drove to Fort Campbell. The family settled into the house the army had assigned to them, and the kids began school. Colin threw himself into his work, knowing that this assignment would take all of his energy. According to the records, his battalions were ranked "dead last." Powell would have to work miracles to fix them.

Two months into 1977, Powell was called to Washington. Jimmy Carter had just been inaugurated as president of the United States, and a new administration was anxious to fill recently vacated jobs. Carter's national security adviser interviewed Powell for a position in the National Security Council. Powell was flattered by the offer but declined it. He wanted to finish out his command at Fort Campbell.

After Powell's command of the Second Brigade came to a close, he was called to Washington again. This time he got two high-level job offers, neither of which he wanted. His goal was to move up from

President Jimmy Carter. When he took office in 1977, he was eager to employ Powell.

brigade commander at Fort Campbell to chief of staff of the 101st Airborne.

But, under the pressure and the advice of friends, Powell caved in and accepted a job at the Pentagon. In May 1977, he became an executive assistant to John Kester, the special assistant to the secretary and the deputy secretary of defense. This was the first of Powell's many advisory positions.

Upon leaving Fort Campbell, one of Powell's commanders, Major General Jack Wickham, said of him: "Colin was the best brigade commander we had. He was best in his tactical knowledge, in his feel for soldiers, and his ability to communicate."

The Powell family left Kentucky and moved back to the Washington area. They had a home built in Burke Center in Virginia's suburban Fairfax County, close to the capital.

Brigadier General at Last!

During the two and a half years Colin Powell spent at the Defense Department, he had an opportunity to travel to the Middle East and Africa. He also received a promotion. In 1979, he was promoted to brigadier general. The promotion from colonel to brigadier general was the dream of a lifetime, and he wanted his entire family to be with him when he received the Silver Star. He had his mother, sister, aunts, uncles, and cousins flown in for the event. Only his dad, who had died a year earlier, was missing.

After Powell's promotion, his name began appearing in national news magazines and became familiar in Washington circles. He took all the attention in stride, waiting patiently for a chance to return to soldiering.

Fort Carson and Fort Leavenworth

When Ronald Reagan became president in 1980, Colin Powell's old bosses—Weinberger and Carlucci—were appointed as defense secretary and deputy defense secretary in Reagan's Cabinet. Colin Powell joined the defense team and served as Carlucci's military assistant until the spring of 1981. By then, he managed to get back into active duty in the army.

Brigadier General Powell became assistant division commander for operations and training, Fourth Infantry Division (Mechanized), in Fort Carson, Colorado. He said good-bye to his White House friends and moved his family to Fort Carson.

After arriving in Colorado, the Powell family began adjusting to a new routine. Mike left in the fall to attend the College of William and Mary in Virginia. Linda entered Cheyenne Mountain High School as a junior, and Annemarie enrolled in Pauline Memorial Academy as a sixth-grader. Alma became active in volunteer work on the post and prepared to use her audiology skills at the hospital.

In July 1982, a little more than a year after coming to Fort Carson, Powell received a call from the

President Ronald Reagan. When his administration took over in 1981, Powell's life changed.

Pentagon informing him that he had been reassigned. He was going to Fort Leavenworth to become the deputy commander general of an operation called CACDA (Combined Arms Combat

Development Activity). His mission was to design a lighter-equipped, smaller infantry division for faster battlefield mobility in Third World conflicts.

Frustrated by the frequent moves, Alma packed up once more, uprooted the girls from their schools, and followed her husband back to Kansas. She found a special surprise waiting for her. There, perched above the Missouri River, was their new home: a historic white mansion on beautifully landscaped grounds. After all the years of living in standard military housing, the Powells had finally struck gold!

Unfortunately, Colin's family had less than a year to enjoy it. On June 29, 1983, Colin was promoted to major general and received his second Silver Star. A month later, after only eleven months at Fort Leavenworth, the Powells returned to Washington. Caspar Weinberger, who had been made secretary of defense in President Reagan's Cabinet, wanted Colin Powell to be his military assistant.

Back to the Pentagon

In July 1983, Brigadier General Colin Powell reported to the Pentagon to serve as Weinberger's senior military assistant. Weinberger was glad to have Powell back on board. Powell worked well with others and got things done quickly. His people skills and organizational skills were invaluable.

Weinberger once said of Powell: "He has excelled in everything he has touched, as he always will. I don't think you can find anyone who has anything bad to say about Colin Powell, which is an extraordinary thing when you've been around Washington as long as he has—in highly sensitive and vital assignments."

Colin Powell learned many lessons about management and politics during his time at the Pentagon. He observed from the sidelines how Pentagon officials responded to military crises in the countries of Lebanon, Grenada, and Iran. Seeing how government worked from the inside profoundly shaped his thinking and his future behavior. After almost three years as Weinberger's military assistant, Powell left politics and returned to soldiering.

On March 26, 1986, he was presented with a third Silver Star to go with his new job as a corps commander. Unfortunately, this time his mother would not be sharing this proud event with him. She had died on June 3, 1984, at the age of eighty-two.

Commander of the U.S. Army V Corps in West Germany

As a three-star general, Colin Powell took command of the U.S. Army V Corps (75,000 troops) in Frankfurt, West Germany. It was something he had always wanted. Later, when recalling this time of his life, he said: "After 28 years of service in the Army, I was probably the happiest general in the world."

Powell's new command was special because his son Michael, twenty-three years old and a lieutenant in the army, was also stationed in West Germany. As a father and as a soldier, Powell could not ask for anything more. When Alma and the girls arrived in West Germany, Second Lieutenant Michael Powell was there to meet them at the airport.

Deputy Assistant to the National Security Adviser

General Colin Powell immersed himself in running the V Corps in Germany. Five months into it, he got a call from Frank Carlucci in Washington. Carlucci had just been appointed head of President Reagan's National Security Council (NSC) and wanted Powell to be his deputy. The NSC advised the president on defense and foreign policy issues.

Frank Carlucci. As head of the National Security Council, he requested that Powell be his deputy.

As a soldier, General Colin Powell had come to expect change. It was a part of a career soldier's way of life. When duty called, he did what he was asked

Colin Powell: U.S. General and Secretary of State

to do. But when duty came calling this time, Powell was afraid it might mean the end of his army career. For a while, Powell managed to resist Carlucci's request to have him work in the White House. But when President Reagan telephoned him personally to say that he needed him, Powell could no longer refuse. He responded as a soldier: "Mr. President," he said, "I'm a soldier and if I can help, I'll come."

Powell's appointment as deputy assistant to the president for national security affairs was announced on December 18, 1986. He flew back to Washington to get a house ready for his family, buy a car, and re-enroll Annemarie in the school she had left five months earlier. Alma remained in Europe to organize the packing and the move. It was not a welcome event. They had moved almost twenty times in the past twenty years!

Rebuilding the NSC

On January 2, 1987, Powell found himself dressed in a civilian suit, sitting in a tiny office in the West Wing of the White House. Next door in a prestigious corner office sat his boss, Frank Carlucci.

Powell had been asked to come on board the NSC to rebuild it and restore trust and confidence in it.

The honesty and integrity of its members had been seriously jeopardized when some of them had become involved in a scandal. In 1984, Congress had passed a law prohibiting U.S. military aid to Iran during its war with Iraq. President Reagan had said that the United States would not assist Iran in the war it was having with Iraq. He also said that the United States would not bargain with terrorists.

But when Iranian terrorists captured Americans in 1985 and held them hostage, a few senior members of the NSC secretly disregarded the law. They sold weapons to Iran in exchange for money and the release of the hostages; the money was channeled to Nicaraguan "contra" guerillas, an action that was also prohibited by law. In 1986, Congress held hearings on the scandal and found Oliver North and John Poindexter guilty of obstructing the law.

After Powell became part of the NSC, he worked closely with Carlucci to restructure it so that none of its members could work independently from one another. They established a chain of command (checks and balances) to prevent a scandal like the one that occurred in 1985–1986 from ever happening again.

A Family Crisis

In June, a family crisis threatened the stability of the Powell family. Colin received news that Michael had been in an automobile accident in Germany. His jeep had gone out of control and flipped over. Immediately, Colin went home to break the news to Alma. That evening they flew to Germany. They found their son in critical condition, suffering from a broken pelvis and internal injuries.

Colin and Alma took Mike back to a hospital in Washington, D.C. There, for the next six months, he underwent several surgeries. With doctors' expert care, and the loving support of his family, Michael recovered and learned to walk with a cane. However, his dream of making a career in the army was over. Shortly after being discharged from the army, Michael married his college girlfriend, and he went on to receive a law degree from Georgetown University.

National Security Adviser

On November 5, 1987, Caspar Weinberger resigned as defense secretary and Frank Carlucci took his place. Colin Powell was the logical choice to replace

The new national security advisor. Caspar Weinberger, President Reagan, and Frank Carlucci joined Powell as he addressed the press.

Carlucci as national security adviser. He knew the inner workings of the organization and was well liked by the president.

On November 5, 1987, Reagan announced Colin Powell's appointment as national security adviser. His choice of the first black-American to hold this position made front-page news all over the United States.

As national security adviser, Colin Powell was at the center of power in Washington. He studied military and political reports, met with secretaries of state and defense, and briefed the president on current world events.

In December, Powell helped plan the summit meetings between President Reagan and Mikhail Gorbachev, leader of the former Soviet Union. For his work on a U.S.-Soviet weapons reduction agreement, he received a Distinguished Service Medal.

In one of many interviews. The press often speaks with Powell about social issues as well as military matters.

THE HEART OF A PATRIOT

Powell left the White House and gave up his position as national security adviser when President Reagan left office in 1989. Before leaving, the president honored Colin Powell for his service to the country with a fourth and final Silver Star.

In 1989, Reagan's successor, President George Bush, offered Powell two positions in his administration: as head of the Central Intelligence Agency (CIA) or as deputy secretary of the State Department. By then, Powell was tired of politics. He thanked the president and respectfully declined the offers. He was proud of the job he had done in the White House, but now he was eager to return to his first love—the army.

Commander in Chief of the U.S. Forces Command

The army appointed Powell as commander in chief of the U.S. Forces Command—known as FORSCOM—headquartered at Fort McPherson, Georgia. As commander in chief of FORSCOM, Powell supervised all army ground forces in the United States, almost a million soldiers (including active-duty, reserve, and National Guard troops). He was constantly on the road, dropping in on the forces from Florida to Alaska. However, when he was not on the road, he came home by 5:30 each evening to a beautiful Victorian mansion. And he and Alma finally had time to enjoy their new status as grandparents. Michael's first child, Jeffrey Michael, had just been born.

Chairman of the Joint Chiefs of Staff

In August 1989, Powell was asked to come to Washington to succeed Admiral William J. Crowe as the chairman of the Joint Chiefs of Staff, the highest military position in the country. Powell was happy with his life at FORSCOM and did not want to move. But he would not refuse President Bush if he wanted him for the job.

President George Bush approved Defense Secretary Dick Cheney's recommendation of Powell and announced his choice in a White House ceremony on August 10. Bush said: "General Powell has had a truly distinguished military career, and he's a complete soldier. He will bring leadership, insight, and wisdom to our efforts to keep our military strong and ready."

Making it official. Secretary of Defense Dick Cheney swore Powell in as the chairman of the Joint Chiefs of Staff.

The Heart of a Patriot

The Senate unanimously approved the president's appointment of Colin Powell on the basis of his leadership skills, his experience in foreign policy, and his high moral standards. He was a proven leader who could communicate with heads of state as well as soldiers in the field.

When Colin Powell moved into his office at the Pentagon, he put two important things on his desk: the marble pen set he had won at Fort Bragg in 1957 for being "Best Cadet, Company D" and a set of "Rules to Live By." The rules were reminders of lessons he had learned over the years. Five of these rules are:

1. It ain't [sic] as bad as you think. It will look better in the morning.
2. It can be done!
3. Check small things.
4. Share credit.
5. You cannot make someone else's choices. You should not let someone else make yours.

Colin Powell was fifty-two years old when he became chairman of the Joint Chiefs of Staff. He was the youngest man ever to serve in this position and the highest-ranking black American in the U.S.

The Joint Chiefs of Staff in 1991. Powell posed with the other military leaders who made up this group.

Army. As chairman, General Powell supervised the army, air force, navy, and marine corps.

The U.S. Invasion of Panama

A little more than twenty-four hours after becoming chairman of the Joint Chiefs of Staff, Colin Powell faced a crisis in Central America. For some time, American officials had known that General Manuel Noriega, head of Panama's military, had been involved in an international drug ring that was pumping illegal drugs into the United States.

Noriega had been working for the CIA and the Defense Intelligence Agency for twenty-five years.

The agencies were paying him for supplying them with information. However, when he was indicted for illegal drug trafficking, the intelligence agencies dropped him from their payroll and the Panamanian people demonstrated against him in the streets. Noriega responded by removing Panama's president, Eric Delvalle, and replacing him with his own man—the education minister.

President Bush wanted to send U.S. troops into Panama to remove Noriega. Colin Powell advised against it. He suggested that the president try negotiating with Noriega first. But when Noriega's troops killed a U.S. marine in a skirmish, Powell proposed a plan to invade Panama and restore it to a democracy. The plan was called Operation Just Cause.

On December 20, 1989, more than 20,000 U.S. troops invaded Panama. It was a swift, full-scale strike. During the battle, twenty-four Americans died and about 300 Panamanians were killed. Later, Noriega was captured and brought to the United States for trial. Eventually, he was found guilty of drug trafficking and sent to prison.

The outcome of the Panamanian crisis confirmed Colin Powell's belief in the benefits of striking suddenly, decisively, and with sufficient force

Leading an invasion. Powell played a key role in Operation Just Cause, which restored democracy in Panama.

to end war. Later, he said in his memoirs: "The lessons I absorbed from Panama confirmed all my convictions over the preceding twenty years, since the days of doubt over Vietnam. Have a clear political objective and stick to it. Use all the force necessary, and do not apologize for going in big if that is what it takes. Decisive force ends wars quickly and in the long run saves lives. Whatever threats we faced in the future, I intended to make these rules the bedrock of my military counsel."

The Heart of a Patriot

The Persian Gulf War

Less than a year after the invasion of Panama, Colin Powell had another military crisis to deal with. The White House received news that 80,000 Iraqi troops, led by President Saddam Hussein, had invaded Kuwait, a neighboring country in the Middle East. The invasion gave Iraq control over Kuwait's valuable oil fields and seriously threatened the borders of Saudi Arabia. The United Nations (UN) responded to Iraqi aggression with economic sanctions—they cut off all foreign trade with that nation.

Colonel Powell preferred the sanctions to military force and advised President Bush to accept the UN decision. The president, however, wanted a military presence in Iraq and began to pressure the UN to authorize force. Although Powell disagreed, he followed the president's orders. Immediately, he and his war staff began to devise a plan to send troops into Saudi Arabia if the Iraqis crossed the border. The plan was known as Operation Desert Shield.

Within a few months, more than 180,000 U.S. troops and a massive amount of supplies and artillery arrived in Saudi Arabia. The presence of the troops and the economic sanctions on Iraq had little effect on Saddam Hussein. He continued build-

American soldiers in Kuwait. In 1990, Powell advised President Bush in ways to control Saddam Hussein of Iraq.

ing up his war machine. In response, President Bush ordered twice as many troops to the Persian Gulf.

On November 29, 1990, the UN Security Council voted 12 to 2 to drive Iraq out of Kuwait. Saddam Hussein was given a deadline for withdrawal. His troops were to be out of Kuwait by January 15, 1991, or the United States would launch an air strike at 3 A.M. on January 17.

From Operation Desert Shield to Desert Storm

By December, Operation Desert Shield, a defensive force, was transformed into Operation Desert Storm,

At a press conference. General Norman Schwartzkopf (right) worked with General Powell during Operation Desert Storm.

an offensive force. General Norman Schwarzkopf, head of the U.S. Central Command in Saudi Arabia, and General Colin Powell made the military plans. From the air, U.S. missiles would destroy the Iraqi communications systems. Then, UN ground troops would cut off Iraqi soldiers from their supplies. Forces from twenty-eight nations took part. And as the deadline approached, the U.S. Congress gave President Bush the authority to go to war.

When Saddam Hussein refused to comply with the UN deadline, Operation Desert Storm began. On January 17, the UN forces led by the United States

Colin Powell: U.S. General and Secretary of State

began the assault on Iraqi troops. It was the largest air strike in history.

Schwarzkopf led the assault from the field. Powell stayed in his Washington office to supervise all communication involving the White House, the military, and Congress. On February 27, 1991 (forty-two days after the war had begun), President Bush declared a cease-fire. By this time, Saddam Hussein was withdrawing his troops from Kuwait. After the victory in the Gulf War, President Bush awarded General Colin Powell the Medal of Freedom, the nation's highest non-military award.

With the war over and American soldiers on their way home, Powell took some time off to relax with his family and celebrate a few important personal milestones in his life. He and Alma were celebrating thirty years of marriage. Their children were now all grown with professional careers of their own. Michael was a happily married man, enrolled in Georgetown Law School. Linda was an actor, debuting in a play on Broadway, and Annemarie was working as a communications specialist in television. For Colin Powell, it felt like one chapter of his life was coming to a close and another one was beginning.

With something to say. General Powell was an important speaker at the 1996 Republican Convention.

RETIREMENT AND NEW BEGINNINGS

During the presidential campaign of 1992, Governor Bill Clinton's campaign staff approached Powell with several job offers. If Governor Clinton were elected president, would Powell be interested in being his vice-president or secretary of state or defense? Powell's answer was no. He was flattered, but he was not willing to accept any political appointment. He preferred to finish out his term as chairman of the Joint Chiefs of Staff and then retire from the army. Colin Powell felt it was time to move on to other things.

When Powell's second term as chairman ended on September 30, 1993, he retired from the army. By then, Bill Clinton had replaced George Bush as president of the United States.

In an emotional farewell, Powell paid tribute to the profession he loved. "I've never in the past thirty-four years found any other line of work, profession, or any other livelihood that appealed to me more than being a soldier," he said. "I am where I am today because the army takes care of its own. I was allowed to rise based on my performance. That is the finest honor a career officer can have."

Then President Bill Clinton paid tribute to Powell. He said: "He clearly has the warrior spirit and the judgment to know when it should be applied in the nation's behalf. . . . I speak for the families who entrusted you with their sons and daughters . . . you did well by them, as you did well by America."

After Colin Powell retired, he was asked what his plans were. He replied, "I'll be busy writing my autobiography [a book about one's life] and I'll be hitting the speech circuit. I'm not going to get involved until I've been out awhile and had a chance to think about how I want to spend the rest of my life. My immediate concern is to make my family financially

Paying tribute. President Clinton had many kind things to say to General and Mrs. Powell.

secure after my thirty-five years on government salary."

Involvement in World Affairs

After retiring, Colin Powell began working on his autobiography. However, he still remained involved in world affairs. On May 10, 1994, President Clinton invited him to join the U.S. delegation to Nelson Mandela's inauguration as president of South Africa. Then on September 15, 1994, Powell accompanied

Around the world. When Nelson Mandela became president of South Africa, Powell attended his inauguration.

former President Jimmy Carter and Senator Sam Nunn on a mission to Haiti. Haitian troops, led by Raoul Cedras, had driven the democratically elected president, Jean-Bertrand Aristide, from office and taken over the government. The UN had authorized the use of force to return Aristide to power. The United States was on the verge of invading the country to make this possible. The Powell-Carter team had come as a last-ditch effort to avoid bloodshed by persuading Cedras to step down.

During an intense meeting with Cedras, Powell described America's overwhelming firepower and convinced him that a good commander would not sacrifice the lives of his soldiers when a mission was impossible. The no-nonsense, military approach worked. General Cedras stepped down and no lives were lost. President Aristide returned to power peacefully.

Writing His Autobiography

Colin Powell spent two years writing his autobiography, which he called *My American Journey*. It was published in September 1995. Afterward, he made a twenty-three-city book tour, then hit the speech circuit. He traveled around the United States talking about things that mattered to him: sacrifice, hard work, pride, and love of family and country.

Powell stressed family values wherever he went, emphasizing how important it is for each family member to look out for the others. Powell referred to America as a big family and the military as a family too. He said: "We've got to start remembering that no member of our family should be satisfied if any member of our American family is suffering or in need and we can do something about it."

Political Offers

In 1995, Colin Powell's political friends began encouraging him to run for president of the United States. He was presidential material, they said. He had worked closely with three presidents and knew what the nation's highest office demanded. He had extensive government experience, knowledge of foreign policy, and a proven record of military successes. Above all, he was a man of character and courage. Americans rated him high in public opinion polls.

Colin Powell thought long and hard about serving as president. After talking it over with his family, he decided it would not be in their best interests. Powell held a press conference to announce his decision: "I have spent long hours talking with my wife and children, the most important people in my life, about the impact an entry into political life would have on us. It would require sacrifices and changes in our lives that would be difficult for us to make at this time. The welfare of my family has to be uppermost in my mind."

When Powell was asked if he thought he could handle the job as president, he said, "Yes. I think I have the skills to handle the job, but I have no political fire in my belly." He went on to say: "Such a life requires a calling that I do not yet hear. And for me to pretend otherwise would not be honest to myself, it would not be honest to the American people. And therefore I cannot go forward." Instead, Colin Powell said he would devote his time to educational and charitable works.

Working for America's Youth

In 1997, Colin Powell became chairman of "America's Promise," an organization that helps young people. Former Michigan Governor George W. Romney created the organization, and the idea was presented at the Presidents' Summit for America's Future on April 19, 1997. Four U.S. presidents endorsed it: Bill Clinton, George Bush, Gerald Ford, and Jimmy Carter.

As chairman of America's Promise, Colin Powell worked with corporations, churches, schools, and

Lending a hand. Powell takes time to work with youth groups and other organizations.

agencies to build and strengthen the health, character, and competence of America's young people. He traveled across the country, stopping at school and community centers to talk to children. His message to America's black children was clear: "Don't let your blackness, your minority status, be a problem to you. If you work hard, do the best you can, take advantage of every opportunity that's put in front of you, success will come your way."

Secretary of State

Colin Powell served as chairman of America's Promise for three years. Then, in December 2000, he answered a new call to serve his country. President-elect George W. Bush, son of former President George Bush, asked Powell to join his Cabinet as he prepared to take office as the forty-third president of the United States.

On December 16, George W. Bush nominated General Colin Powell as his secretary of state. In January 2001, the U.S. Senate confirmed the nomination, and General Colin Powell became the country's sixty-fifth secretary of state. He is in charge of all U.S. foreign affairs, and he is the spokesman for the United States around the world.

Living a Successful Life

Colin Powell has proudly served three presidents in the White House and now, as secretary of state, he is serving in a fourth administration. He has fought bravely for his country's honor. Through it all, he has been successful in every job he has undertaken.

To those who ask Colin Powell for his secret of success he says: "There's no substitute for hard work and study. People keep asking what is the secret to

Giving advice and inspiration. General Powell is often invited to speak to groups throughout the nation.

my success. There isn't any secret. I work hard. I spend long hours. I don't get distracted from the task before me. It's as simple as that."

For Colin Powell, success has always been as simple as that: discovering what you want in life, setting goals, studying, working hard, and giving back through service. His past accomplishments have always proved that. We can be sure that Colin Powell's future successes will also be the result of those simple facts.

TIMELINE

1937   Colin Powell born in Harlem, New York, on April 5

1958   Graduates from City College of New York as ROTC distinguished military graduate

1959   Completes first army tour of duty; becomes platoon leader; is promoted to first lieutenant

1962   Marries Alma Johnson; is promoted to captain

1963   Completes first tour of duty in Vietnam; is injured by enemy booby trap

1966   Is promoted to major

1968   Completes second tour of duty in Vietnam; receives Soldier's Medal for bravery

1969   Returns to Washington, D.C., to attend master's degree program at George Washington University

1970   Is promoted to lieutenant colonel

1972   Becomes White House Fellow working at the OMB

1974   Completes tour of duty in South Korea

1976	Is promoted to colonel
1979	Is promoted to brigadier general
1982	Takes command at Fort Leavenworth, Kansas
1983	Is promoted to major general; becomes military assistant to Secretary of Defense Weinberger
1986	Is promoted to lieutenant general; becomes commander of V Corps in Frankfurt, Germany
1987	Serves as deputy to National Security Adviser Carlucci; becomes national security adviser
1989	Is promoted to full general; becomes chairman of the Joint Chiefs of Staff; manages Operation Just Cause in Panama
1990	Manages Operation Desert Shield
1991	Manages Operation Desert Storm
1993	Retires as chairman of the Joint Chiefs of Staff and from the army
1994	Forms part of an American delegation to restore elected government to Haiti
1995	Publishes autobiography, *My American Journey*; considers running for presidency in 1996
1997	Becomes chairman of America's Promise
2000	Speaks at the Republican National Convention to nominate George W. Bush as president of the United States
2001	Becomes secretary of state under President George W. Bush

HOW TO HAVE A CAREER IN THE MILITARY

Background

Five separate military services make up the United States armed forces: the Army, Navy, Air Force, Marine Corps, and Coast Guard. These services organize, train, and equip the nation's land, sea, and air services to support the national and international policies of the U.S. government. Together, they are responsible for the safety and protection of the citizens of the United States. Those who choose to be members of the armed forces dedicate their lives to protecting their fellow Americans.

America's earliest organized defense forces were the militias of the colonial states, which began to come together in the first decades of the seventeenth century. More than 100 years later, in 1775, the Continental Army was established to fight the British in the Revolutionary

War. The colonists so valued the Continental Army that its commander, General George Washington, became the first president of the United States.

With the Japanese surprise attack on Pearl Harbor, Hawaii, in 1941, America was plunged into World War II. At its height, 13 million Americans fought in the military services. When the war ended, the United States emerged as the strongest military power in the Western world.

In the years following World War II, the United States and its allies devoted their considerable military resources to fighting the Cold War with the Soviet Union. Anticommunist tensions led to U.S. involvement in the Korean War during the 1950s and to participation in the Vietnam War, which ended in the mid-1970s. Antiwar sentiment grew increasingly insistent, and the policies that established an American presence in foreign countries soon came under new demands for re-evaluation. In 1973, the draft was abolished, and the U.S. military became an all-volunteer force. The armed forces began to put great energy into improving the image of military personnel and presenting the military as an appealing career option, in order to attract talented recruits.

During the 1980s, the U.S. military increased its efforts to bring about the collapse of Soviet Communism and became active in the Middle East, particularly in the Persian Gulf, through which flowed much of the world's oil supply. Later in the decade, many countries under Soviet rule began to press for independence, and, in 1991, the Soviet Union finally collapsed under the weight of its political and economic crisis, effectively ending the Cold War. That same year, the United States engaged in the successful Persian Gulf War.

In recent years, a new role has developed for the U.S. military as a peacekeeping force. Much of America's future military efforts will be influenced by the United Nations and will involve cooperation with the armed forces of its allies. Today, American troops are stationed in the Balkans to discourage renewed aggression in a long-standing civil war. Other active forces continue to monitor the Persian Gulf. In the years to come, military service personnel can expect additional active duty of this type.

Structure

The general structure of the military is pyramidal, with the president of the United States acting as the commander in chief of the U.S. armed forces. The president's responsibilities include appointing top military officers and maintaining the nation's military strength.

The secretary of defense is an appointed position usually awarded to a civilian. He or she is a member of the president's Cabinet, presiding over the Department of Defense and directing the operations of all military branches. The Joint Chiefs of Staff—the senior commanders of the different services—work with the secretary of defense to advise the president on military matters.

Together—under the guidance of the Department of Defense—the army, navy, air force, marine corps, and coast guard comprise the armed forces. The goals of all five branches are similar: the defense and protection of U.S. citizens, territory, and interests at home and around the world.

The army is the senior service. It is traditionally known as the branch that fights on land. Most of the nation's more than 25 million living veterans served in the army, and the army continues to be the largest of the services in total recruits, with 444,000 personnel in 1999.

The navy, more than any of the other services, has a special way of life. Guided by traditions of the sea, it is more of a closed society in many ways than other services. Its officers and enlisted people work and live together at sea for long periods—a lifestyle that demands close attention to duties and teamwork. Ships and aircraft units visit many parts of the world. It can be an unusual and wonderful life, and strongly appealing to many who are looking for a different and exciting type of career. In 1999, there were approximately 281,000 navy personnel.

The air force, newest of all the services, is highly technical and appeals to those interested in aviation and mechanical trades. Approximately 343,000 personnel were employed by the air force in 1999.

The marine corps operates on land and sea, and marines usually form the advance troops in military operations. The corps is closely associated with the navy, and like the navy, prides itself on meeting the highest possible standards in training, military bearing, and discipline. Apart from more military duties, marines provide security on navy property, and guard U.S. Embassies and Consulates around the world. There were approximately 143,000 marine corps personnel in 1999.

With approximately 26,000 personnel in 1999, the coast guard is the smallest of the military services, and, as such, offers unique opportunities. It is responsible largely for the enforcement of maritime law, but is perhaps best known for its involvement in search and rescue efforts, aiding those in distress at sea. Although opportunities exist for overseas assignments, most coast guard jobs are related to the waters and shores of the United States. Positions in the military fall under two broad occupational categories: enlisted personnel and officers. Enlisted persons carry out the daily operations of the military and are considered noncommissioned officers. Commissioned officers function as managers of the military, overseeing the work of the enlisted personnel.

In addition, both the army and navy maintain a third classification of skilled experts called warrant officers. Enlisted soldiers or civilians who demonstrate technical and tactical ability in any one of several dozen occupational specialties may qualify as a warrant officer. Warrant officers are highly specialized, and gain additional expertise by operating, maintaining, and managing the services' equipment, support activities, or technical systems throughout their careers. Specialties include, but are not limited to, missile systems, military intelligence, telecommunications, legal administration, and personnel.

A broad general difference between the requirements for enlisted personnel and officers is academic preparation. While the service branches accept applicants of varying ages and educational backgrounds, officers are required to have college degrees, while enlisted people are not. Those who intend to serve as enlisted personnel should finish high school and then enlist. High school graduates are more likely to be successful in the military than nongraduates, and the services accept few applicants without a high school diploma. All service applicants must take the Armed Services Vocational Aptitude Battery (ASVAB) as a requirement for enlistment.

All service personnel receive special training in military skills. Those who want to rise in the ranks will have the opportunity to attend school or undertake independent study and will be rewarded with advancement. Military education in many instances is related to civilian occupations, an added incentive for those who later may decide not to make a career of military service.

While many recruits enter the armed forces immediately after graduating from high school, the military uses every opportunity to advance the education of its recruits. Frequently, service members in both categories—both officers and enlisted men and women—obtain undergraduate and advanced degrees on their own initiative while in the service. The range of educational possibilities is diverse and often exciting, and financial help for study at outside institutions is readily available. You can learn to operate the engineering equipment of an aircraft carrier or, with appropriate academic qualifications, proceed through medical training to become a military physician. With a serious sense of commitment and a great deal of rigorous preparation, you even can join the navy's SEALS program, or "get jets," and become a member of the Blue Angels.

"Within the ranks," so to speak, each military branch has nine enlisted grades and ten officer designations. The names of ranks vary among the services. This is why a simple numbering system has been adopted to denote rank. Promotion depends on your ability, the number of years you've served, and the length of time since your last promotion. On average, a diligent enlisted person can expect to earn one of the middle noncommissioned or petty officer ratings; some officers can expect to reach lieutenant colonel or commander. Outstanding individuals advance beyond those levels.

The pay for the equivalent grades in all services is the same. It starts comparatively low for new recruits but increases—on a fairly regular schedule—to a more substantial salary for top officers and enlisted people. Congress sets the pay scales after hearing the recommendations of the president. In addition to basic pay, hazardous duty pay may be earned by enlisted personnel who frequently and regularly participate in combat. Other special allowances include special-duty pay and foreign-duty pay.

The services also supply without charge many basic necessities that must be paid out of pocket in most civilian positions, such as food, shelter, and health care. Military men and women receive a number of additional benefits. They include access to recreational facilities, free medical and dental care, schools for dependents, financial advice, legal assistance, and religious support.

Military people may apply for retirement after twenty years of service. Generally, people retiring from military service will receive 40 percent of the average of the highest three years of their base pay. This rises incrementally, reaching 75 percent of the average of the highest three years of base pay after 30 years of service. The widow or widower of a service member who died on active duty or after a service-connected disability discharge will receive, for life or until remarriage, a monthly payment computed on the basis of the rank of the deceased spouse. The surviving spouse also receives disability insurance. All retirement provisions are subject to change, however, and should be verified before you enlist.

At about age forty, a person is still in the prime of life for most work, and although the retirement pay is comparatively good, military retirees generally choose to start new careers in civilian life. Military training usually has prepared a person for a related trade or profession, and many military people look forward to early retirement. They view it as an excellent opportunity to take a civilian job and keep the financial cushion of military retirement pay. Others, of course, prefer to stay in the service longer, perhaps for their entire working lives; generally speaking, only the more senior service members have that opportunity. Even in retirement, service people are subject to recall in times of national emergency.

Outlook

Before you consider a career in the armed forces, it's important to remember that a military life is regimented. As a service member, you may not always be able to choose your assignments, your place of work, or your home. Your responsibility is to serve your country and your military unit, so the needs of your country and the service come first. The modern services try hard to give members what they want—a good worker gets special consideration for the same reason a civilian employer rewards a top employee. But most service members at some time will, for example, work on the East Coast when they would rather be on the West Coast; go to sea when they would rather stay home; live in a house or barracks on the base when they would rather have an apartment in town; or serve a year in a post abroad when they would rather be with their families.

In contrast to personal sacrifices such as these which

are asked of service members, it's heartening to remember that the country always will need a military, both for defense and to protect its interests and citizens around the world. It's true that over time, often because of political or economic influences, the requirements necessary to meet these needs change. As America's position in the world grew stronger in the early 1990s, for example, the military engaged in a major "downsizing," reducing personnel in nearly every branch and at all levels. Recently, however, the size and strength of each service has reached a "steady state," and the armed forces now must work to combat the public misperception that military jobs are not as available as they once were. Contrary to current public opinion, opportunities for a career in the military services continue to be plentiful. Department of Defense statistics show that more than 186,000 new recruits joined a branch of the armed forces in fiscal year 1998, and at least two services—the army and navy—failed to reach recruitment targets.

The primary barrier to earning a position in the armed forces is no longer job availability. Instead, educational requirements and advancement standards continue to be raised as military jobs become more complex and technologically advanced. Because of the many benefits of military service, including college tuition grants and specialized training, competition for military positions may be expected to rise. The prospects for promotion for officers also will become more competitive. Opportunities for enlisted positions will become more limited for those without a high school diploma. Applicants with some college education have the best prospects.

TO LEARN MORE ABOUT MILITARY CAREERS

Each of the military services publishes handbooks, fact sheets, and pamphlets describing entrance requirements, training and advancement opportunities, and other aspects of military careers. For more information, contact the following offices or your local recruiter. Each service command office can be emailed directly through its Website.

Air Force Recruiting Command
Randolph Air Force Base
550 D Street West, Suite 1
San Antonio, TX 78150
210/652-3104
http://www.airforce.com

Army Recruiting Command
Fort Sheridan, IL 60037
800/USA-ARMY
http://www.dtic.mil/armylink

Coast Guard Information Center
4200 Wilson Boulevard, Suite 450
Arlington, VA 22203
1/800-GET-USCG
http://www.dot.gov/dotinfo/uscg

Marine Corps Recruiting Command
3280 Russell Road
Quantico, VA 22134-5103
703/784-9433
http://www.hqmc.usmc.mil

Navy Recruiting Command
801 North Randolph Street
Arlington, VA 32203
800/USA-NAVY
http://www.navy.com

HOW TO BECOME A GOVERNMENT OFFICIAL

The Job

Federal and state officials hold positions in the legislative, executive, and judicial branches of government at the state and national levels. They include governors, judges, senators, representatives, and the president and vice president of the country. Government officials are responsible for preserving the government against external and domestic threats. They also supervise and resolve conflicts between private and public interest, regulate the economy, protect the political and social rights of the citizens, and provide goods and services. Officials may, among other things, pass laws, set up social-service programs, and decide how to spend the taxpayers' money.

Nearly every state's governing body resembles that of the federal government. Just as the U.S. Congress is composed of the Senate and the House of Representatives, every state except Nebraska has a senate and a house. The president and vice president head the executive branch of the U.S. government, while the states elect governors and lieutenant governors. The governor is the chief executive officer of a state. In all states, a large group of officials handle agriculture, highway and motor-vehicle supervision, public safety and corrections, regulation of intrastate business and industry, and some aspects of education, public health, and welfare. The governor's job is to oversee their work. Some states also have a lieutenant governor, who serves as the presiding officer of the state's senate. Other elected officials commonly include a secretary of state, state treasurer, state auditor, attorney general, and superintendent of public instruction.

Besides the president and vice president of the United States, the executive branch of the national government consists of the president's Cabinet. The Cabinet includes the secretaries of state, treasury, defense, interior, agriculture, and health and human services. These officials are appointed by the president and approved by the Senate. The members of the Office of Management and Budget, the Council of Economic Advisors, and the National Security Council are also executive officers of the national government.

State senators and state representatives are elected to represent various districts and regions of cities and counties within the state. The number of members in a state's legislature varies from state to state. The U.S. Congress has 100 senators as established by the Constitution—2 senators from each state—and 435 representatives. (The number of representatives is based on a state's population.) The primary job of all legislators, on both the state and national levels, is to make laws.

Requirements

High School   Courses in government, civics, and history will help you gain an understanding of the structure of state and federal governments. English courses are also important. You need good writing skills to communicate with your constituents and other government officials. Math and accounting will help you develop the analytical skills needed to understand statistics and demographics. Science courses will help you make decisions concerning health, medicine, and technological advances. Journalism classes will help you learn about the media and the role they play in politics.

Postsecondary   State and federal legislators come from all walks of life. Some hold master's degrees and doctorates, while others have only a high-school education. Although most government officials hold law degrees, others have undergraduate or graduate degrees in such areas as journalism, economics, political science, history, and English. No matter what you majored in as an undergraduate, you'll likely be required to take classes in English literature, statistics, foreign language, Western civilization, and economics. Graduate students concentrate more on one area of study; some prospective government officials pursue a master's degree in public administration or international affairs. Take part in your college's internship program, which will involve you with local and state officials, or pursue your own internship opportunities. By contacting the offices of your state legislators and your state's members of Congress, you can apply for internships directly.

Other Requirements

Good "people skills" will help you make connections, gain election, and make things happen once you are in office. You should also enjoy argument, debate, and opposition—you'll get a lot of it as you attempt to get laws passed. A calm temperament in such situations will earn the respect of your colleagues. Strong character and a good background will help you avoid the personal attacks that occasionally accompany government office.

Exploring

A person as young as sixteen years old can gain experience with legislature. The U.S. Congress, and possibly your own state legislature, has opportunities for teenagers to work as pages. They want young people who have demonstrated a commitment to government study. If you work for Congress, you'll be running messages across Capitol Hill, and you'll have the opportunity to see senators and representatives debating and discussing bills. The length of a page's service can be from one summer to one year. Contact your state's senator or representative for an application.

Become involved with local elections. Many candidates for local and state offices welcome young people to assist with campaigns. You'll make calls, post signs, and get to see a candidate at work. You'll also meet others with an interest in government, and your experience will help you gain a more prominent role in later campaigns.

Employers

State legislators work for the state government, and many hold other jobs as well. Because of the part-time nature of some legislative offices, state legislators may hold part-time jobs or own their own businesses. Federal officials work full-time for the Senate, the House, or the executive branch.

Starting Out

There is no direct career path for state and federal officials. Some stumble into their positions after some success with political activism on the grassroots level. Others work their way up from local government positions to state legislature and then into federal office. Those who serve in the U.S. Congress have worked in the military, journalism, academics, business, and many other fields.

Advancement

Initiative is one key to success in politics. Advancement can be rapid for someone who is a fast learner and is independently motivated, but a career in politics usually takes a long time to establish. Most state and federal officials start by pursuing training and work experience in their particular field, while getting involved in politics at the local level. Many people progress from local politics to state politics. It is not uncommon for a state legislator to eventually run for a seat in Congress. Appointees to the president's Cabinet and presidential and vice presidential candidates have frequently held positions in Congress.

Work Environment

Most government officials work in a typical office setting. Some may work a regular forty-hour week, while others work long hours and weekends. One potential drawback to political life, particularly for the candidate running for office, is that there is no real off-duty time. The individual is continually under observation by the press and public, and the personal lives of candidates and officeholders are discussed frequently in the media.

Because these officials must be appointed or elected in order to keep their jobs, it is difficult to plan for long-range job objectives. There may be long periods of unemployment, when living off savings or working at other jobs may be necessary.

Frequent travel is involved in campaigning and in holding office. People with children may find this lifestyle demanding on their families.

Earnings

In general, salaries for government officials tend to be lower than salaries in the private sector. For state legislators, the pay can be very much lower. According to the NCSL, state legislators make $10,000 to $47,000 a year. A few states, however, don't pay state legislators anything but an expense allowance. And even those legislators who receive a salary may not receive any benefits. However, a state's top officials are paid better: The Book of the States lists salaries of state governors as ranging from $60,000 to $130,000.

The Congressional Research Service publishes the salaries and benefits of Congress members. Senators and representatives are paid $136,673 annually. Congress members are entitled to a cost-of-living increase every year but don't always accept it. Congressional leaders such as the Speaker of the House and the Senate majority leader receive higher salaries than other Congress members. For example, the Speaker of the House makes $171,500 a year, and U.S. Congress members receive excellent insurance, vacation, and other benefits.

Outlook

To attract more candidates for legislative offices, states may consider salary increases and better benefits for state senators and representatives. But changes in pay and benefits for federal officials are unlikely. An increase in the number of representatives is possible as the U.S. population grows, but it would require additional office space and other costly expansions. For the most part, the structures of state and federal legislatures will remain unchanged, although the topic of limiting the number of terms a representative is allowed to serve often arises in election years.

The federal government has made efforts to shift costs to the states. If this trend continues, it could change the way state legislatures and executive officers operate in regards to public funding. Already, welfare reform has resulted in states looking for financial aid in handling welfare cases and job programs. Arts funding may also become the sole responsibility of the states as the National Endowment for the Arts loses support from Congress.

The government's commitment to developing a place on the Internet has made it easier to contact your state and federal representatives, learn about legislation, and organize a grassroots movement. This increase in voter awareness of candidates, public policy issues, and legislation may affect how future representatives make decisions. Also look for government programming to be part of cable television's expansion into digital broadcasting. New means of communication will involve voters even more in the actions of their representatives.

TO LEARN MORE ABOUT GOVERNMENT OFFICIALS

Books

Bonner, Mike. *How to Become an Elected Official.* Broomall, Penn.: Chelsea House, 2000.

Fish, Bruce, and Becky Durost Fish. *The History of the Democratic Party.* Broomall, Penn.: Chelsea House, 2000.

James. Lesley. *Women in Government: Politicians, Lawmakers, Law Enforcers.* Austin, Tex.: Raintree/Steck-Vaughn, 2000.

Lutz, Norma Jean. *The History of the Republican Party.* Broomall, Penn.: Chelsea House, 2000.

Websites

Congress.Org

http://www.congress.org/

A guide to Congress, providing information about House and Senate members as well as current bills and legislation

U.S. House of Representatives
http://www.house.gov
Provides information about the House of Representatives

U.S. Senate
http://www.senate.gov
Information about senators and how the Senate works

Where to Write
National Conference of State Legislatures
1560 Broadway, Suite 700
Denver, CO 80202
303/830-2200
For information about *State Legislatures Magazine*, and other information concerning state legislatures

U.S. House of Representatives
Washington, DC 20515
202/224-3121

U.S. Senate
Office of Senator (Name)
United States Senate
Washington, DC 20515
202/224-3121

TO LEARN MORE ABOUT COLIN POWELL

Books

Blue, Rose. *Colin Powell: Straight to the Top.* Brookfield, Conn.: Millbrook Press, 1997.

Passaro, John. *Colin Powell.* Chanhassen, Minn.: The Child's World, 2000.

Patrick-Wexler, Diane. *Colin Powell.* Austin, Tex.: Raintree Steck-Vaughn, 1996.

Schraff, Anne. *Colin Powell: Soldier and Patriot.* Springfield, N.J.: Enslow Publishers, 1997.

Wukovits, John F. *Colin Powell.* Minneapolis: Lucent Books, 2000.

Websites

America's Promise

http://www.americaspromise.org/

For information about the organization Powell headed for three years

Colin Powell Speech
http://www.robtshepherd.tripod.com/powell.html
Excerpts from Powell's speech at the Republican National Convention

The Powell Factor
http://www.time.com/time/magazine/archive/1995/950710/950710.cover.html
Time magazine cover story from 1995, profiling Powell and his possible run for the presidency

Interesting Places to Visit
The Freedom Museum
10400 Terminal Road
Manassas, VA 20110
877/393-0660
A Smithsonian affiliate dedicated to twentieth-century military efforts

The Pentagon
Washington, DC 20301-1400
703/695-1776
To tour the headquarters of the U.S. Department of Defense

Unites States Military Academy
West Point, NY 10996
845/938-4011
The premier institution for those interested in U.S. Army careers

INDEX

Page numbers in *italics* indicate illustrations.

ABOUT THE AUTHOR

Alice Flanagan lives in Chicago, Illinois, and writes books for children and teachers. Ever since she was a young girl, Ms. Flanagan has enjoyed writing. Today, she has more than seventy books published on a wide variety of topics. Some of the books she has written include biographies of U.S. Presidents and First Ladies; biographies of people working in our neighborhood; phonics books for beginning readers; informational books about birds and Native Americans; and career education in the classroom.